ISBN 978-1-332-74448-0
PIBN 10220159

This book is a reproduction of an important historical work. Forgotten Books uses state-of-the-art technology to digitally reconstruct the work, preserving the original format whilst repairing imperfections present in the aged copy. In rare cases, an imperfection in the original, such as a blemish or missing page, may be replicated in our edition. We do, however, repair the vast majority of imperfections successfully; any imperfections that remain are intentionally left to preserve the state of such historical works.

1 MONTH OF
FREE
READING

at

www.ForgottenBooks.com

By purchasing this book you are eligible for one month membership to ForgottenBooks.com, giving you unlimited access to our entire collection of over 1,000,000 titles via our web site and mobile apps.

To claim your free month visit:

www.forgottenbooks.com/free220159

THE

National Geographic Magazine

Vol. VII   NOVEMBER, 1896   No. 11

THE WITWATERSRAND AND THE REVOLT OF THE UITLANDERS *

By George F. Becker,

United States Geological Survey

The South African Republic, or, as it is more often called, The Transvaal, lies in southeastern Africa, between the Limpopo or Crocodile river on the north and the Vaal river on the south. Portuguese and British possessions shut it off from the Indian ocean on the east, and the country to the north and west of the republic is also British. The Vaal river is tributary to the Orange, which flows into the Atlantic, while the Limpopo empties into the Indian ocean. The watershed between these rivers is the Witwatersrand, or white-water-range, which trends nearly east and west about south latitude 26°, and is therefore only 150 geographical miles from the tropic of Capricorn.

The Transvaal may be roughly described as an elevated plateau, most of which lies between 4,000 and 6,000 feet above sea level. To the north of the Witwatersrand the general level is not much over 4,000 feet. Immediately to the south of this watershed, near Johannesburg, the elevation is about 6,000 feet, gradually diminishing toward the Vaal. The general aspect of the country reminds one of the Laramie plains, but the rainfall averages about 30 inches, and the climate is mild and equable. The soil is only moderately fertile, and 15 years ago the country was considered fit for nothing but pastoral occupation.

The Witwatersrand, in the neighborhood of Johannesburg, consists of upturned edges of a thick mass of quartzites, shales, and conglomerates, known as the Lower Cape formation. These

* Paper read before the National Geographic Society, October 16, 1896.

23

rocks are of Paleozoic age, but carry no fossils. The conglomerates of this group almost all contain more or less gold. The most famous mines of the Transvaal are opened upon a certain set of these conglomerate beds known as the Main Reef series. Resting unconformably on the Lower Cape is another group known as the Upper Cape and containing one bed of conglomerate, the Black Reef, which has been profitably worked for gold at some points. An extensive sheet of dolomite forms one member of the Upper Cape. Unconformably on the Upper Cape lies the Triassic, carrying very extensive beds of coal, one of the treasures of the Transvaal of which little is heard outside of South Africa. As the country is also rich in iron ores, one may expect to hear more in the future than in the past of these coal fields. Meantime they supply the gold-mining industry with good and cheap fuel. The Lower Cape formation, with the Main Reef series, is exposed only to a limited extent. Within less than 20 miles of Johannesburg, both to the east and west, the Upper Cape and the Triassic beds flood the country, and for a long distance only an occasional glimpse is to be had of the Lower Cape with its auriferous conglomerate. It is said by various engineers to reappear occasionally for hundreds of miles from Johannesburg—as, for instance, in Zululand—and to be more or less auriferous wherever found. It need hardly be remarked that the search for the Main Reef beneath the Trias is most arduous. That it will eventually be traced far beyond the surface exposures of the district is quite certain.

In this paper the Witwatersrand district alone is of especial interest, but in conveying a general notion of the Transvaal it must be remarked that this is by no means the only auriferous district in the republic. There are four other districts, containing in all ten mines, which yield at the rate of over $100,000 each annually. Of these the Klerksdorp district carries gold in conglomerates. In the three other districts the gold is found in ordinary veins. The Sheba mine, in the De Kaap district, has yielded over $5,000,000. Four of the important mines lie in the Lydenburg district, and one, the Sutherland, in the Zoutpansburg district. The total gold product of the Transvaal for 1895, outside of the Witwatersrand, was $3,581,000, while the Rand alone yielded $38,110,000.* Statistics show that the yield of the outside mines is increasing about as rapidly as that of the Rand.

* For comparison it may be noted that the United States produced in 1895 $46,610,000 worth of gold, or about $4,900,000 more than the Transvaal.

The great gold deposits of the Rand are beds of conglomerate, known in South Africa as " banket " or " reef." They crop out for some 27 miles at a distance of from one to two miles from the crest of the Witwatersrand, and usually dip near the surface at an angle of 45° or more. When followed downward the dip diminishes somewhat rapidly to 25° or less. None of the mines are yet very deep; none in fact reach 2,000 feet, but the reefs have been found by the diamond drill to a depth of 2,500 feet. The structure of the country seems to show that below the 2,000-foot level the reefs will continue for a long distance at a moderate angle. How deep mining can be carried on may be more or less questionable, but the mining engineers on the Rand confidently believe that they can get down 5,000 feet, and I agree with them. The ore of the Rand is phenomenally uniform for an auriferous deposit. While it is locally patchy, considerable areas show only moderate fluctuations from a general average. The quantity of gold can be computed with something like the same confidence that the amount of coal in a coal seam can be calculated. Such a computation is in the nature of things only a first approximation, but within certain limits it has a value. Estimates of this kind for the whole area or portions of it have been made by various experts, among whom may be mentioned Mr Hamilton Smith, Bergrath Schmeisser, of the Prussian mining service, Mr John Hays Hammond, Messrs Hatch and Chalmers, and Professor De Launay, of the Paris School of Mines. These estimates accord fairly well. The latest is Professor De Launay's, who, after a review of the other estimates, calculates by a method of his own that to a depth of 1,000 meters (2,381 feet) and for a length of outcrop of 25 miles the amount of gold accessible is 13 or 14 milliards of francs, or from 2,600 to 2,800 million dollars. This would give down to the 5,000-foot level from 3,962 to 4,267 million dollars. Other of the estimates, similarly treated, would give still larger values. Hatch and Chalmers, on the other hand, estimate that the Rand proper, together with outlying portions of the district (all within about 20 miles of Johannesburg), will yield down to the 5,000-foot level about 3,500 million dollars. I have not been able to find any grounds for regarding this as an overestimate, and I know of no one familiar with the deposits who thinks it exaggerated.

The sketch of the character and resources of the Transvaal just given contains nothing new. It has been outlined in order to indicate how it happens that a community has suddenly sprung up at Johannesburg, composed of enterprising, highly intelligent, and perhaps somewhat impatient men, hailing from many different lands—men as different as possible from the pastoral pioneers who compose the South African Republic. The Boers and the foreigners, or "Uitlanders," as they are called in Dutch, were not congenial and the great mining camp has all along constituted a menace to the peace of the Republic. As every one now knows, the threatened danger was not averted.

The dramatic incidents which have taken place in the Transvaal during the past ten months have drawn the attention of the whole world to that country. The interest in these events felt in the United States has been little less intense than that in Great Britain. This is entirely natural, for many of the leading men in Johannesburg are Americans; indeed, the mining industry is chiefly under the guidance of American engineers, and the United States was represented on the reform committee by seven members. It really behooves the American public therefore to know how prominent American representatives of an important profession have behaved themselves under trying circumstances. While there is a natural sympathy in the United States for Anglo-Saxons taking up arms for their rights, we, as Republicans, also sympathize with the South African Republic in the endeavor to maintain its independence. This fellow-feeling makes it all the more interesting and important to examine carefully and, if haply such a thing is possible, impartially as well as carefully, into the causes and conduct of the revolt.

I wish this inquiry had fallen into other hands than mine, but I happened to visit the country in April for a stay of some months; several of the condemned men are old friends of mine as well as colleagues, it naturally fell to my part to make such efforts in their behalf as I could, and still in spite of these personal relations it is clear to me that there is much to be said on the Boer side of the questions at issue. So far as opportunities go, therefore, I am perhaps in as good a position as any one can be to review the circumstances without prejudice. The great difficulty in this, as in any inquiry of an historical nature, is to ascertain the facts, for these are differently represented by different though seemingly well-informed persons. I trust it will be found that I have measurably succeeded.

It would be impossible to understand the conditions which led to the grievances of the Uitlanders without considering some of the influences which have made the Dutch colonists or Boers what they are. The Boers are most closely related to us ethnologically, but their political and industrial history has been so different that jealousies and antagonisms have arisen which, though highly regrettable, are by no means without excuse.

The Boers, like the English, are in the main of Teutonic blood, with a relatively small infusion of French stock. Like the English, they are stubborn, self-reliant, fond of the chase, and admirably adapted to cope with the difficulties incident to colonization in a country occupied by savage beasts and still more savage men. The Boer ideal seems to be life on a large estate, with plenty of sport and the occupation of not too exigent stockbreeding and farming. So far their tastes do not differ greatly from those of many Englishmen, but they are for the most part ignorant of the refinements of life so dear to advanced Anglo-Saxons, and perhaps on this account they are almost devoid of the commercial instincts through which such tastes might be gratified. They are, it is said, usually able to read print, but for the most part their reading is confined to the Bible. They are highly religious, and the Bible appeals to them as to few other peoples, because the scenery and material conditions of the Book are so similar to those by which they are surrounded. The very animals are the same. Their religion is somber and puritanical; it is that of the Old Testament, with little sweetness or mercy in it. Under normal conditions the Boers are generously hospitable and they are brave. It is true that Englishmen have sometimes reviled them as cowardly, but their whole history, and particularly the battles of Boomplaats and Majuba Hill, shows the contrary. The accusation seems to be due in part to the fact that like all continental Europeans they are greatly averse to fisticuffs, and partly to the fact that in fighting with rifles they avail themselves of cover whenever they can. Taking advantage of cover I understand to be a well-established principle of all modern tactics.

Many of them are said to be untruthful, at least in matters of business. This is not strange, for it was long ago observed that financial responsibilities do more than the most stringent religion or than amiability and bravery to foster a high standard of truthfulness. The Boers are sometimes spoken of as a degenerate race, but this is certainly a slander. They usually possess an excellent physique, and it is perfectly well known that one or two generations of education put the Dutch colonist

on a par with men of any nationality. The struggle for exist-
ence and for freedom has saved them from mental stagnation.
That they are backward as a race, according to our standards,
is true. Much of the seventeenth century still clings to them,
but they have lost none of the capacity for advance.* The
most important of all the characteristics of the Transvaal Boer
is his passion for freedom or, what in his case is tantamount to
the same thing, his horror of British domination. In 1880 the
women of the Transvaal urged their sons and husbands to arms,
bidding them die like patriots, if need were. This passionate
horror of English rule is an historical development. The Boers
have had little opportunity to observe how mild and beneficent
English rule can be under certain circumstances.

Cape Colony passed into the possession of the British Crown
by force of arms in 1806, and was formally ceded by the Prince
of Orange in 1814. The white population of the Cape at that
time consisted of the descendants of Dutch colonists and French
Huguenots. The latter had found their way to Africa through
Holland after the revocation of the Edict of Nantes in 1685. At
no time did the Huguenots exceed one-sixth of the colonists, or,
if the Dutch East India Company's servants are counted, one-
eighth of the total European population. The colonists had
little intercourse with Europe during the 18th century. Like
other colonists of the time, they owned slaves, their lives were
pastoral and agricultural, and, except for the Bible, their studies
were confined to woodcraft. The petty impositions of the Dutch
East India Company had made them unscrupulous so far as
transactions with the government were concerned ; the incorrigi-
ble carelessness of Hottentot servants had weakened the habits
of cleanliness which they had brought from Holland, and the
possession of slaves had produced its usual deleterious effects.

* Mr John Nixon, in his Story of the Transvaal, 1885, which certainly cannot be ac-
cused of partiality to the Dutch colonists, says : "I have the pleasure of numbering
many intelligent and educated Boers among my acquaintance, and I desire to put on
record my opinion that a 'good' Boer is quite equal to a good Englishman. Nay, in
one respect he is better, for he adds to the virtues of an Englishman an unbounded
and generous hospitality. . . . The educated Boer is a splendid stock. . . . No
one can deny that on that day [Majuba] the Boers fought bravely and well."

The Uitlanders commonly form an extremely unfavorable opinion of the Boer.
They do not desire Boer hospitality and they see nothing of his qualities as a pioneer,
while in business they find him suspicious, untrustworthy. and behind the age; but it
would not be fair to judge of a people like the Boers entirely from a commercial
standpoint. The Boer, on the other hand, is not without justification for suspecting
English designs on his independence, and he can point to many promises of the
British government which have not been fulfilled ; but it is not fair to judge a people
like the English entirely from a political standpoint.

Thus, except in the resources appropriate to pioneers, they had been left behind in the march of civilization.

The British colonial policy in the early decades of this century had not yet developed into its modern phase of mildness in any part of the world. In 1815 took place a little disturbance which has been designated by the exaggerated name of the " rebellion " of Slachter's Nek.* Two of the insurgent Boers and one Hottentot British soldier only were killed, yet the British punished the revolt by hanging five men, none of whom had shed a drop of blood, while thirty-two others were condemned to banishment, imprisonment, or fines. This cruel sentence, followed by no commutation, has never been forgotten by the Boers, and small is the wonder. The use of the Dutch language was forbidden in the courts of Cape Colony in 1827, and for a short time those who did not understand English were even disqualified from jury duty. In 1834 the slaves were emancipated suddenly by act of Parliament. The compensation proposed was only one-third of the appraised value, and the conditions of obtaining this fraction were so onerous that the colonists in many cases realized only a fifth or a sixth of the actual value, and sometimes nothing at all. Many families were reduced to want, and great misery was caused by the injudicious execution of a measure the principle of which was laudable. The emancipated negroes were placed on a political equality with their recent masters, and the government refused to pass vagrant laws to control the blacks. This was a period when philanthropists were very enthusiastic on the subject of the universal brotherhood of man, and it was supposed by many well-meaning people that Kaffir tribes were intrinsically on a par with white communities. The Boers knew better. Their refusal to acknowledge the equality of white and black drew down on them the wrath of the missionaries, who were extremely influential both in London and Cape Town. There seems to be no doubt that the Dutch were represented as far more cruel to the natives than they really were, while the blacks were painted as far less barbarous than they are known to have been.† Thus the mutual antagonism of the Boers and the English was fomented by the apostles of peace.

* The origin of this affair was the refusal of a Boer named Bezuidenhout to comply with a summons to answer a charge of having ill-treated a colored servant. There seems to have been no politics in it.

† That some terrible cruelties have been perpetrated by the Boers on the blacks during periods of hostility is not to be doubted. It must be remembered that white prisoners taken by the blacks were and are tortured with indignities sickening to hear of and quite indescribable in print.

The various grievances briefly indicated above led to the first great " Trek," or emigration of the Boers, from Cape Colony in 1836–'37. Taking only their herds and such movables as they could load on their wagons, thousands left the country. The emigrants themselves maintained that they left the colony not to avoid law, but lawlessness, and they made it evident that their chief motive was to escape the severe yet inefficient English domination. In a manifesto by one of their principal men, Peter Retief, written in 1837 it is asserted, " We quit this colony under the full assurance that the English government has nothing more to require of us and will allow us to govern ourselves without its interference in the future." Vain hope!

In migrating into the wilderness, the Boers naturally came into contact with the natives, not the negroes of the United States, who came from the West Coast of Africa, nor the Hottentots of the Cape, but the great Bantu or Kaffir race, which includes the Zulus, Matabili, Basutos, etc. These people are of a dark bronze hue, and have good athletic figures. They possess some excellent traits, but are horribly cruel when once they have smelled blood. The Bantus appear to have reached the cape about the same time as the Europeans, killing out Hottentots and Bushmen as they advanced, and waging furious inter-tribal wars. Again and again a Bantu tribe, effectively organized under some able chief, has swept a great region clear of human beings. When their witch-finding ceremonies are considered as supplementing the unsparing slaughter of war, it is remarkable that any considerable number of Bantu remained. Nothing but the phenomenal fecundity of the race has kept up its numbers.

The trekking Boers thus met tribes who held their territories only by the right of recent and bloody conquest and to whom battle was the object of life. If the Boers had small compunction in taking land from them, it is perhaps not to be wondered at. The Boers paid for it, like the Bantus, with blood. The history of the conflicts between the Boers and Zulus is wildly romantic. It has been written and cannot be repeated here.

The greater part of the territory occupied by the South African Republic and by the Orange Free State was absolutely depopulated by the Matabili (or rebel Zulus) under Moselekatse in 1817. Twenty years later this chief and his followers fled to the north of the Limpopo river, as the result of independent defeats by the Zulu subjects of Dingaan and by the Boers.

When they left Cape Colony a portion of the Boers settled in

ZULU BRIDE AND BRIDEGROOM

Natal, after the loss of a great part of their number, treacherously slaughtered by the Zulu chief, Dingaan. The English had repeatedly refused to annex Natal, but after the Boers had been settled there for five years and had set up a republic, the British took possession, and to escape them most of the Boers trekked again to the north of the Orange river, where many of their kinsfolk had preceded them in 1836–'37. Repeated official declarations had been made that the British dominion would not be extended to the northward of this river. Nevertheless, in 1848, British sovereignty was proclaimed over the region between the Orange river on the south and the Vaal on the north, practically the area now occupied by the Orange Free State. The Boers resisted the annexation; two of their number were hanged and the property of other recalcitrants was confiscated. As early as 1842 many Boers had entered the Transvaal. After the annexation of the country to the south, many more crossed the Vaal. In 1852 the population amounted to about 5,000 white families, and the independence of the Transvaal was acknowledged by England in the Sand River Convention.

In 1877 the Transvaal was annexed by England on the plea that the weakness of the state was a menace to English interests.* But the unwillingness of the Boers to be British subjects had not diminished, nor were they without grave reasons for dissatisfaction. It is acknowledged by men of all parties that the promises made by the English at the time of the annexation were not kept.† Late in 1880 the republican flag was again hoisted; war and the battle of Majuba hill followed, and in 1881 the Transvaal was again acknowledged independent,‡ though with the reservation of British suzerainty. In 1884 the relation of the two countries was further modified by a convention, which is still in force. In this document the only substantial right reserved to Great Britain is that of ratifying treaties between the republic and foreign powers.

An attempt has been made in the foregoing paragraphs to show the origin of the hostility and distrust with which the Boers regard the English, but it is not to be inferred that the

---

* Proclamation of annexation and address of Sir T. Shepstone. The annexation was nominally provisional. In 1879 Sir Garnet Wolseley announced that it should continue "forever."

† Mr Nixon writes: " Nor were any of the other promises which were expressed or implied at the time of the annexation carried out."

‡ The greater part of the above historical notes are taken from Mr G. McC. Theal's History of South Africa. 4 vols. Mr Theal is generally acknowledged to be a trustworthy and impartial historian.

British policy in South Africa has been one of consistent and deliberate oppression. Vacillating it has been, through changes in party government, through ignorance in the colonial office of conditions in South Africa, and through the idiosyncrasies of arbitrary or doctrinaire commissioners. Many of the British governors have lost reputation and have been recalled in consequence of their mistakes, but South Africa has gained little by the penalties meted out to her rulers. In public affairs enlightened wisdom is more useful than virtue; for wrongs, though unintentionally committed, can seldom be righted or even fully atoned for.*

Gold had been discovered in the Transvaal in the Lydenburg district as early as 1867, and prior to 1881 it had been found at other points as well, but none of these discoveries were of a very sensational character. The marvelous deposits of the Witwatersrand were detected in 1885.

The Witwatersrand as a gold-producing district has no parallel in history. It is now producing from an area no larger than the District of Columbia at the rate of more than $40,000,000 worth of gold annually, and, as has been mentioned, there are good reasons for believing that the ultimate total production will be approximately $3,500,000,000, or about ten times the total value of the product of the Comstock lode.† Production did not begin till 1887. Of course, Johannesburg, the chief town of the district, grew with the utmost rapidity.

A census of the district within three miles of Market square was taken in July last. It showed 51,225 whites and 51,849 colored people. Doubtless the enumerators missed some residents, but probably no large proportion of them.

The sudden development of this vast industry naturally produced a profound effect upon the financial circumstances of the Transvaal, although the Burghers did not take part in the exploitation of gold. The Boers sold land at enormous valuations, furnished transportation at high rates, sold produce at famine prices, and levied most profitable taxes. How greatly they bene-

---

* The loyalty of many Englishmen is so extreme that they esteem it a blessing for any people to come under English domination, whether willingly or otherwise. They cannot understand how people can prefer independence to the British rule. This fact explains many instances of aggression which to an American seem without excuse.

† As estimated by the Mint Bureau of the United States, the Comstock produced up to January 1, 1896, about $149,000,000 worth of gold. If silver is reckoned at the coining value, or $1.2929 per fine ounce, the total product of the lode is estimated at $357,472,626.85. The gold is about 42 per cent of the total value. Last year the production of this great lode fell below a million dollars.

fited by the mining industry from a pecuniary point of view is illustrated by the fact that the public revenue in 1894 was six times that in 1886. The Boers did not foster the foreign com-munity on the Rand, in spite of its beneficial influence upon their finances. On the contrary, they held aloof, and actually threw many obstacles in the way of the progress of the industry. They evidently regarded the immigration as a new and insidious form of British invasion. The independence which they had achieved by remarkable efforts and sacrifices was jeopardized by a peaceful inroad, and they were in danger of losing their free-dom by a process of absorption into a larger community growing in their own midst.

That they should resist this new form of conquest by every means available to them was inevitable. Indeed, any other course would have belied their entire history. The most evident means of retaining control of their own destiny was to render the acquirement of the franchise difficult if not impossible, and this perhaps indispensable measure was promptly taken.

So far as I can learn, both the liberal or progressive party and the conservative or Dopper party of the republic are in accord as to the policy of practically denying the franchise to foreigners. On other points they differ. The conservatives, who are repre-sented by the present administration, do not include among their members a sufficient number of educated and professional men to fill the offices rendered needful by the new order of things. They cannot draw largely on the opposition to fill these places, and few of the Cape Boers, being British subjects, are available for the execution of the anti-English policy.* Hence it is to Holland that President Kruger is almost forced to turn for edu-cated men of Dutch speech to carry out the Dopper program. The railway, too, from Delagoa bay to Johannesburg and other points in the Transvaal is in the hands of the Netherlands Rail-way Company,† a fact which tends greatly to increase the influ-ence of the Dutch in the Transvaal. It would also seem to be a deliberate plan with the conservative party to offset and mini-mize English influence as far as possible by that of the Nether-lands, from which the republic has nothing to fear.

* According to Mr Wessels, in a lecture delivered in 1894, the fear of betrayal to Eng-land is frankly stated as a sufficient reason for not appointing Cape Boers to office in the Transvaal.

† The concession for this road was originally conferred under President Burgers in 1875, but the road was only completed so as to connect with the Cape system in 1894. It is said to be the most profitable railway in the world. The republic has the right to take possession of it.

The Dutch, or, as they are called in South Africa, the " Hollanders," are not popular with the progressive party, which could fill many of the offices with its own members. Neither is it the policy of this party to foster the influence of the Netherlands in the republic. The liberal party, as I gather, holds that so long as the control of the country is retained to the Burghers by limiting the franchise, any undue influence of the English can be obviated with little aid from Europe.* The mining community detests the Hollanders, for it is through them that nearly all the obstructive policy of the government is carried out. It is charged that the Hollander officials are very corrupt, and that some of them are so is certain. It is not, however, to be supposed that all of these members of an honorable nation are bad,† and that many of them are able is beyond question. Dr Leyds has shown himself a statesman of a very high order. Among the assistants he has chosen there must be many intelligent enough to appreciate the expediency of honesty. That bribery exists, however, and that mining companies bribe on a large scale is certain. Bribes are said to be indispensable.

It may be suspected that a large part of the Hollanders are in Africa to make their fortunes, with the intention of returning to Europe when this end is accomplished. If so, they are most undesirable officials or even burghers. No man of ordinary virtue who does not identify himself with the country in which he lives, to whom that country is not " home," will use official power or the franchise consistently for the best interests of a community from which he longs to be gone.

The Uitlanders of the Rand were, and are, extremely discontented under the Dopper policy of exclusion, obstruction, and repression. They considered themselves superior to the Burghers and a benefit to the country, and they were indignant at the favor shown to the Hollanders. They desired to manage local affairs in their own way, and above all to be unobstructed in the accumulation of wealth and in the development of the mining industry. The way to attain these desires which most naturally suggested itself to the Anglo-Saxon mind was to obtain the franchise on terms similar to those exacted in English colonies and in the United States. It is not clear that any large portion of

* At the last presidential election, in 1893, Mr Kruger was elected by a majority of only 843 over General Joubert, the progressive candidate and now Vice-President, in a total vote of 14,944.

† Mr Wessels says that among the Hollanders you will find " worthy descendants of a race that can boast of Egmont and Horn, of Hugo de Groot and Olden Barneveld."

CROSSING THE UMKELOSI RIVER, SWAZILAND

the English and American residents were attached to·the Transvaal in the sense of regarding it as a permanent home. Most of them meant or hoped to return to Europe or America, and it is probable that even had the full franchise been obtainable after five years' residence, few Anglo-Saxons would have abjured allegiance to England or the United States.* It was for business purposes that they desired a voice in public affairs, and few of them realized that, to the Boers, granting the franchise seemed equivalent to self-destruction.

So far as I can learn, the great mistake of the Boers was in giving the Uitlanders grave cause for desiring to control the legislation affecting them and the industry they had built up. The Uitlanders could have been quieted by judicious consideration for their convenience, without the franchise and without danger to the independence or the national character of the republic. A prosperous community like that of the Rand would· bear extremely heavy taxation with little murmuring; but a prosperous and energetic community is the very last to submit patiently to discomfort, favoritism, and maladministration beyond its own control.

The grievances of the Uitlanders have been very real indeed, and the foreigner on the Rand has not been allowed to forget for an hour at a time that he was a member of an ill-governed community. A few facts will illustrate this condition. The town of Johannesburg, though containing over 50,000 white inhabitants, has no perfected system of lighting, no system of drainage, and no general water supply. There is abundance of water in the neighborhood, but the law of riparian rights, being framed for a purely agricultural population, is such that no water rights can be acquired if a single affected landowner objects. The town has no general municipal government, though there is a board of health. The state has refused until lately to aid education, except when conducted in Dutch. Public meetings of more than six persons may be dispersed at the discretion of the police. The charges of the Netherlands Railway Company are entirely uncontrolled by law, and on a portion of its line its tariff reaches the utterly exorbitant rate of six cents per ton per mile on coal. The company makes profits of 100 per cent, and yet it is not taken over by the state, which has the legal right to assume its ownership. No dynamite is made in the Transvaal, yet a mo-

---

* It is probable that a considerable number of Africanders would naturalize if the conditions were not too onerous. The Burghers, however, dread the influence of the "English-minded" Africander.

nopoly of its sale has been granted to a company which pays the government something over five shillings per case and charges the miners 85 shillings, of which about 36 shillings is profit. Other concessions of a like character have been threatened, though not carried out as yet. Until August, 1896, the government insisted upon allowing grog-shops accessible to the blacks to be kept open in the immediate neighborhood of the mines and mills, with lamentable results. There is no commission or any body of officials charged with the general administration of the district to whom appeals can be addressed or from whom assistance can be obtained. Taxation is so arranged as to fall almost exclusively on the Uitlanders, and it has not been reduced, although the treasury has a large surplus and although there are no industries to be protected. Many of the officials with whom the Uitlanders come in contact are open to bribery and, it is alleged, will not act except when paid to do so.

It is easy to imagine how very seriously business was and is hampered by these abuses. No fair-minded person can avoid sympathizing with the exasperation of capitalists or mine managers at the needless difficulties thrown in their way and the unjust exactions laid upon them. Enterprising and determined men could not be expected to submit tamely to such conditions, and it is not wonderful that resentment should have carried them beyond the limits of prudence or moderation. In considering the grievances, however, it will be apparent that they bear as a whole much more heavily on capitalists and business men than on employés. White miners, machinists, and mining engineers have almost without exception received higher pay and also made more money on the Rand during the last few years than ever before or in any other region. The direct personal discomforts to which they have been subjected have not been greater than they would have undergone in the mining camps of the United States or of Australia, all of which are much smaller than this. Thus it cannot be denied that the direct and tangible grievances are mainly capitalists' grievances and that the revolt is a capitalist revolt. The employés in joining the movement were influenced by a sense of irritation due to needless deprivation and discomfort and the knowledge that the source of their prosperity was endangered by oppressive exactions.

It is quite obvious that these causes of complaint could be removed by the exercise of a little of the good judgment with which the executive is abundantly supplied. The problem is vastly less difficult than those with which President Kruger and Dr Leyds have successfully grappled during the past few months. This district might be governed by commissioners and a judiciary appointed by the president of the republic, almost precisely as the District of Columbia is administered. The efficiency of such an administration would depend only on securing able and honest men, and it is absurd to doubt that the Transvaal can secure the services of such. The present tyrannical oppression of the Rand disgraces a people to whom no sacrifices were too great for the attainment of their own freedom. They should be the first to appreciate the hardships under which the Uitlanders are suffering, and to show the value they themselves put on liberty by imposing no unjust restraints upon others.

The Uitlanders made repeated efforts, by passing resolutions and presenting petitions, to obtain the franchise and the redress of grievances. These efforts extended over several years, but they met with no success. During the closing months of 1895 the agitation for reform was accentuated. The discontent of the Uitlanders was at this stage fomented under the guise of sympathy by residents of other portions of South Africa with a view to creating disturbances in the republic for ulterior ends. The idea was broached of making an armed demonstration, which it was hoped might impress the Boers sufficiently to bring about the desired changes. This seemed possible, because the Uitlanders are supposed to number about 50,000 men and the Boers only about 25,000 * adult males.

The plan of threatening the government with force of arms was unfortunate from its very inception. Many of the Uitlanders felt that while the grievances were sore, they were not great enough to justify armed revolt, and these men withdrew from the movement. The seceders were chiefly those least susceptible to the influence of the purely English element in South Africa, viz., the Germans and a few Frenchmen. The bad feeling and even alienation arising from this defection is not yet allayed. The split in the Chamber of Mines, which is now unfavorably affecting business, was one of its results. While the Boers were fully equipped, the foreigners were almost unarmed, and the importation of arms is under legal restrictions, originating in the necessity of limiting or suppressing the sale of guns to the blacks. To procure arms in any quantity, therefore, it was necessary to

---

* This is Mr Charles Leonard's estimate. The Boers on that basis must count a total population of something like 125,000. The Uitlanders in the republic are very largely bachelors and probably number something like 75,000 men, women, and children.

smuggle them. A few thousand were brought in secreted under coke. A portion of these arms was forwarded by members of the British South Africa Company, better known as the Chartered Company. An arrangement was also made with Dr Jameson, and it has been alleged at his suggestion, that if matters were to go wrong at Johannesburg and the Boers should attack it the Chartered Company's administrator should come to the rescue with a body of men who as a matter of fact were chiefly policemen of the company.

The National Union had formed no plot against the independence of the republic, their idea being either to frighten the administration into granting redress of grievances or at most to substitute forcibly a more liberal administration for the present one. Such an administration would treat commerce more generously and stimulate trade with Cape Colony. This, in the opinion of the Uitlanders, would sufficiently repay Dr Jameson, if, indeed, he required reward for coming to the rescue of his countrymen and countrywomen in case of need.

The union issued a manifesto, defining its demands, on December 26, 1895. On the 30th news was received that Dr Jameson had crossed the border, contrary to agreement and in spite of requests on the part of the leaders of the union to remain beyond the boundary. The same day the reform committee was formed expressly because, as the notice to members states, Jameson's crossing the border " renders it necessary to take active steps for the defense of Johannesburg and the preservation of order." Before dawn on the morning of the 31st the leaders received information that on Jameson's arrival the British flag would be hoisted. This was portentous news for all parties. Without any consent on their own part, the reformers were made partners in an attempt at conquest instead of reformation. For the Americans the situation was particularly grave. For an American to assist in overthrowing a republic in order to aggrandize a monarchy would be to forfeit all respect from his countrymen. There is not the slightest evidence that any one of the seven Americans on the committee either contemplated such a crime or welcomed the situation thrust upon them. Mr John Hays Hammond, the only American among the leaders, took the appropriate step as soon as possible after daylight. He hoisted the Transvaal flag and he both demanded and obtained an oath of allegiance to it from the members of the reform committee, some eighty in all; but for this fortunate action the trial of the reformers in April

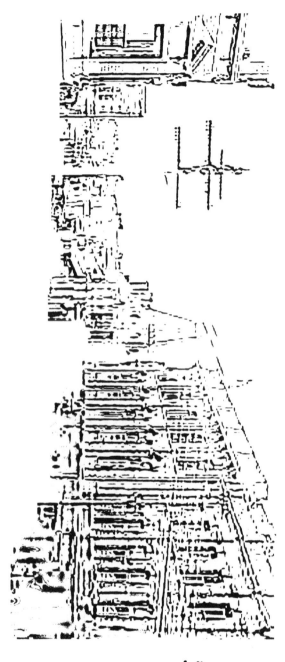

would have had more serious consequences. I am not aware that any member, either American or English, demurred to the oath.

The reform committee was a direct and inevitable consequence of the arming of the Uitlanders, coupled with Jameson's invasion. The Boers could not be expected to understand on the spur of the moment that Jameson had invaded the country in contravention of a distinct agreement. The Uitlanders were therefore from the Boer point of view engaged in an attempt to conquer the country; they were public enemies and subject to attack. Knowing this, and not knowing whether the Boers would exercise any forbearance, it seemed needful to the Uitlanders to organize themselves for self-defense.

In the rank and file of the reform committee there were six Americans. Messrs T. Mein, Joseph Story Curtis, and Victor Clement are well known, both in the United States and in Africa, as mining experts and managers; Mr Charles Butters is a metallurgist who has had remarkable success in improving the chemical treatment of gold ores; Mr H. J. King is a partner in the mine-owning firm of S. Neumann & Co., London, and Mr F. R. Lingham is a timber merchant. These men joined the committee very rashly, it is true. They did not know to what extent the Uitlander party had become implicated in treasonable procedures, nor did they stop to inquire. They assumed that nothing further was involved than organization for self-defense, and signed their names without adopting any of the precautions which they would have exercised in putting their signatures to any business documents of relatively trifling import. Of carelessness they certainly cannot be acquitted, but I have not been able to ascertain, either from Uitlanders or Burghers, that there is the slightest shadow of implication in real treason resting on any one of these Americans. Many of the Englishmen associated with them were equally guiltless. It is now easy for the dullest to see that the Americans would have been wiser to take no part in the Uitlanders' revolt. In those December days, on the other hand, it was very difficult to steer an even course over the boiling tide of events, avoiding the headland of Rashness and the maelstrom of Pusillanimity. If some of our men went ashore, they have taken their mishap like men; there has been no attempt to shift the blame and no whining over the issue. Their conduct, at any rate, has been such as we expect, and have a right to expect of Americans.

Every one knows that the revolt ended in a dismal fiasco. The

24

Transvaal government was evidently prepared for the invasion. Jameson and his troopers were captured with all their documents and even the key to their cipher dispatches. The Johannesburgers laid down their arms, and most of the reform committee were arrested. At their trial, in April, four of the leaders,[*] including Mr Hammond, pleaded guilty, on advice of counsel, to high treason, and the remainder pleaded guilty to lese majesté,[†] excepting Mr Curtis, who was detained by illness in Cape Town. His trial was postponed. The leaders were condemned to death on April 28, but the next day their sentence was reduced to fifteen years' imprisonment. The rank and file of the reform committee were given terms of imprisonment ranging from a few months to a couple of years. For some weeks no further mitigation of sentence was announced, and during this interval the government took occasion to publish telegrams and maps captured from Jameson's party, showing how deliberate had been the plot to deprive the republic of its independence. Such of the mass of the reformers as signed a petition for mercy were then discharged, on payment of a fine of £2,000 each. Two of them only, both Englishmen, refused to sign any appeal for clemency, and these gentlemen, whose attitude seems to most people a mistaken one, still remain in jail, so far as I am informed. Early in June the leaders also were released, on payment of the heavy fine of £25,000 each. . They were given permission to remain in the Transvaal on condition of signing a pledge not to meddle in the affairs of the republic. This Colonel Frank Rhodes refused to do, and he was promptly escorted to the border. Mr Curtis, when sufficiently recovered from a very dangerous illness, presented himself in July for trial, but refused to plead guilty. The government, however, declined to proceed against him under plea of not guilty, evidently because it was loath to reopen the whole disagreeable question. I understand that Mr Curtis has contributed £2,000, the amount his comrades were fined, to the charities of the Transvaal, not caring to take pecuniary advantage of his exceptional position.

The surrender of Dr Jameson and his officers to the British

* Mr Charles Leonard, one of the five leaders, left the country before the arrest of the reform committee   The other leaders were Messrs George Farrar, Lionel Phillips, and Frank Rhodes.

† The prisoners understood that there was an understanding between their counsel and the prosecution that the plea of guilty would be followed by a mild sentence. This arrangement is wholly denied by the prosecution and, according to Reuter, by counsel for the defense. I have not been able to ascertain the origin of the misunderstanding. A trial would have resulted in much ill-feeling, and it is as well that it was avoided.

authorities by the government of the Transvaal and their subsequent trial in London need not be dwelt upon. The leader was condemned to fifteen months in prison, without special privileges, but he was shortly afterward granted the status of a first-class misdemeanant as an act of clemency. So far as I could learn, the sentences passed on the raiders were regarded in the Transvaal as adequate but not excessive. The share of Mr Cecil Rhodes and of the Chartered Company in responsibility for the raid is still to be investigated.

Quiet once more reigns in the Transvaal. The Uitlanders are again pressing for reforms, but there is no thought of revolt. The Burghers are now alive to the need of reforms, and as they seem anything but vindictive, I believe they will gradually concede what a sense of justice demands.

The Reformers, though very able men in their own professions, have been mere puppets in the hands of men whose designs were much larger and more dubious than the correction of the Uitlanders' grievances. The honest soreness of the foreigners over their wrongs was taken advantage of to excite them to a rebellion not justified by the provocation. The Transvaal government showed little business ability in giving or tolerating even a shadow of excuse for rebellion, but in the active contest which followed it displayed an astuteness for which the ability of its enemies was no match. The union of South Africa under British hegemony, for which Mr Rhodes has labored so persistently, seems further off than ever. The Transvaal burghers are substantially Dutch ; so are the citizens of the Free State ; so, too, are four-fifths of the Cape Colonists. The bond of sympathy between the Boers throughout South Africa has been drawn much closer during the past few months. The Africander League in Cape Colony, which aims at "Africa for the Africanders", *i. e.*, practically for the Boers, is much stronger than it was, and the whole race now sees in the Transvaal, which is arming to the teeth, an intellectual ability to cope with the larger questions of politics which has not hitherto been available. It seems today as if the position of the South African Republic in this region were very much like that of Prussia in the divided Germany of forty-one years ago. The whole country is in a state of tension, and a blundering policy on the part of the Paramount Power might have unusually serious consequences. Thus South Africa will probably command a larger measure of interest and attention from the world henceforth than hitherto.

CPSIA information can be obtained
at www.ICGtesting.com
Printed in the USA
BVHW041520250219
541084BV00012B/1476/P